AS LONG AS I LIVE

ALL ABOUT POETRY

GRACE

Every challenging work needs self efforts as well as guidance of elders especially those who were very close to our heart.

My humble effort I dedicate to my sweet and loving

Family and Friends,

Whose affection , love , encouragement and prays of day and night make me able to get such success and honor.

Along with all hard working and respected

Teachers

Special thanks to mimo and tia for always listening to me and supporting me. I want you to know how much I love and appreciate you. You're the best!

Contents

Contents

Contents

me

One day all my poems will reach the right place

either in someone's heart or in a beautiful book...

water

Let the joys and sorrows of life

yours and mine

mingle like waters from two rivers

and then ,

it would be difficult to seperate your existence from mine

just as no one can draw a line on water

raindrop's

Life is an unending desert of seperation

but your words fall like raindrop's on the sands of my soul

these raindrop's comfort me

I see in your eyes

In your eyes , I see

The relish of the wind,

The freshness of the morning,

The brightness of the noon ,

The exquisite evenings ,

And the hushed nights..

I see in your eyes

The road

I took the road less travelled

the loneliness of the woods was calming ,

the silence was comforting,

the chirruping of the birds soothing.

I walked miles to reach joy's lake ,

but the clear water made me awake,

I craved for your essence,

The beautiful wilderness called for your presense

Name of life

Offer yourself to bring a smile to someone

share a shoulder to bear someone's pain,

have love for someone in your heart,

this is the name of life

life is great when it's sacrificed for love.

I have faith in this even when no one else has..

because

This is the name of life

A poet I am not

A poet I am not, but

O'beau

Since the day I saw you,

poetry I came to know

A dancer I am not, but

O'beau

Since the day I saw you,

dancing I came to know..

A gardner I am not,

but O'beau

Since the day I saw you

I planted seeds of love in my heart..

A priest I am not ,

but O'beau

Since the day I started loving

I was as if I began worshiping..

A poet I am not ...

Without you

As if the sky without colors,

as if the flowing wind

without a fragrance ,

like some viel without shame,

like the act of bowing to God

without a prayer ,

without you , i am that way

Night of pain

The matter is now beyond control

The state of the heart is returning to normal

Now the madness is getting beyong limits

and the self is getting consoled

Uncounted messages have gone

and the light breeze now blows

for a moment..

O stars, now go and sleep

the night of pain is nearly over..

Lamp of my dreams

Somewhere far away

when the day dwells

the dusk sneaks up,

shyly like a bride

In the courtyard of my imagination

someone lights up the

lamp of my dreams..

Epitomizes

You are the light in the night,

I am the darkness in the day

You are a sacred vessel

I am a damp wood

The story of my defeat,

The tomb of my passionate love,

the rokes of my heart full of thorns ,

everything epitomizes my being..

Lines of fate

What's the point of this kind of meeting

being together yet lonely

Once again , my heart has given me this curse

On these lines of fate ,

why have you written seperation ...

Stranger among strangers

Beneath my bare feet is

a path of burning coal..

All my life I have lived

a stranger among strangers

Oh! please

Take me to the place you call home

for this ignorance world

wishes to be my enemy..

Marks

The day.. When

sky bow down to land

two worlds will meet

Happiness of meeting will be everywhere

Bridal vehicle will be decorated

Fragrances will be everywhere

God himself will come as an officiant

From all directions , the nights will tell our story

The songs of our love

will be repeated by the generations...

One day

I won't be here,

You won't be here,

Yet , our marks will be left...

Path

The heart says the path is difficult

Don't know where is the destination

From this point, there go different paths,

Some leisurely , some fast paced

Some paths leading to stately mansions, others to glass houses

Some to nests of weeds ,

all go from this path..

That voice drowned

Going far off, slowly that voice drowned

Only memories remained

He went away

And it was difficult for her

to conquer those distances..

Whenever she turned back to look
she couldn't see his face

In the echoing past, she could only hear

'My name will be lost,

but my thoughts are my identity,

only if you can remember'

The stars smiled

The moon bloomed

the stars smiled

the night is surprisingly tipsy trill

see those roads sparkled with moonlight are

beckoning as they sway.

The moon rays spread their arms

and our desires dance and sway

strings of heart strummes

the milieus crooned

let this love bloom in life at its will..

The web of stars

bring out my heart

don't ask how my heart now feels..

This is all I have to tell you

Whether I remain there or not

Just remain there

somewhere in me..

when I get my last sleep ,

keep coming in my dreams..

This is all I have to tell you

Someday if there is a rain

think that I am there in the drops.

If the sun troubles you

in the morning

know that I am in the rays..

Whether I say something

or not,

just keep listening to me,

This is all I have to tell you..

Smile

What is the sorrow that

you are hiding under your smile?

there is wetness in your eyes

but smile on the lips,

what's your condition

and what you are trying to show it as..

If you keep drinking these tears,

they'll become poison for you ,

those wounds that the time

has almost healed,

why are you keeping on disturbing them..

Evening

You're like the day,

I'm like the night

Now let's get together

like the evenings..

Oh! My heart was never as careful as now

We walk on empty roads

with our eyes closed

ending up in a faraway place.. Aimlessly!

Autumn

It was autumn then, no?

The rustling whisper's of leaves

falling in autumn..

I had bought back those

whisper's once by wearing them as earrings

A branch of autumn still trembles

in the breeze..

Make that branch fall down,

and return all thosmemories to me

As if

As if some request is hidden in your heart

As if you have said something through eyes

As if a lifetime has passed while we stayed awake

As if there is still life but the breath has stopped

As if your eyes are asking me something

While walking down a path,

I get this feeling

As if you are secretly watching me

As if a moment contained in it a journey of ages

As if the life is passed by us very fast

I think about you everytime like this

As if my every breath was for you..

Dream

This misty night,

these joyful winds

and that beautiful moon,

rising slowly

Why is the moonlight silent

after kindling a fire

within me

This signal of the weather

doesn't even let me sleep..

this flaunty wind,

and the sapphire like sky,

there is a dew of intoxication on the buds,

Even in such a beautiful weather,

why is the heart restless,

I don't know what is missing in life

the one I could not find in the light of the day,

the heart looks like a dream ..

lost in the shimmer of this night ,

I'm searching for myself...

In such a time, is there no one

who would remember me

even by mistake?

one who would fulfill

the world of my dreams

with a simple smile..

A story about you and me

A song of love it is,

a flow of joy it is

Life is nothing more

but a story about you and me

From a life of a couple moments,

have to steal a whole lifetime..

Life is nothing but a story

about you and me

You are a stream of river

while I am yoir shore,

In my eyes there is an ocean

and also waters of desires..

The storm is certain to happen

and destined to disappear as well..

This is a cloud of few moments and soon

it has to pass away..

shadows remain, marks remain..

You are here?

Is this a gust of wind

or your fragrance

Is this a moonlight

or are my nights damped by your eyes

Is this the soft rustling sound of the leaves

or did you whisper something

I'm quietly thinking about this

since a long time

and when I know that

you are not here,

nowhere around

but why this heart is saytng that,

you are here

somewhere around here

Those days

It's the same shower of rain today

It's the same fire

which has ignited in my heart..

Those days were something like this only,

when we had met..

When the flowes had blossomed in our hearts..

It's the same weather ,

but the times are not the same..

Now even the rain cries with me

I wish someone puts a hand on my heart,

and put the pieces of this heart together,

But then these are all thoughts and dreams,

has anything broken ever become complete again...

Sorrow

This the my reality

I'm controlled by It's strings

My eyes lay upon them

and I see their lives

Full of brokenness

My heart decieves me

For better It lies, then to accept It's fruits

My hands , they bare their iniquity

The bitter taste of truth

From this cup I must drink

I have sculpted this monstronity

Oh! how the darkness scares me ,

but it feels like home

Alone

Alone

Alone

Journey of thorns

The dried flowers

that is closed in a book

make it dust,

If somewhere someone

talks about me ,

call it a mistake

but let that be a mistake

that doesn't displease you,

that,If you sleep,like me

You too have no peace

for a moment..

In a corner of some drawer,

I found your picture..

Once again, It's that journey of thorns,

In that street of flowers..

At least tell me your name

What would you know

of how anxious this heart is for you?

What would you know

of what kind of dreams this heat dreams?

If you are here,

my heart hopes that this fleeting moment still

that the river of time,

ever flowing

Freeze at this sight...

You have made this heart insane

can it be blamed?

Oh - ocean - eyed

At least tell me your name!

O, so what if today I am far from you?

so what if I am unknown to you?

If I cannot have you,

so what if you remain a mere desire?

These are desires

May there be no clamour

May there be gatherings of silence

May there be no one in this world

May we be alone

I am dreaming of you

What else do I have to do anymore?

Oh- ocean-eyed

At least tell me your name!!

What shall I do?

This heart settles on none else

but you,

what shall I do?

Only you tell me , my faithful sweetheart,

what shall I do?

In a stolen heart a lamp

cannot be lit,

what shall I do?

To settle in someone's heart

and then to torment it

To show someone glimpses of self

and then hide

To allow the garden of hopes

to wither..

At times heart feels the weight of shadows

Thousand woes exist in this world,

own and of others

the sorrows of love are not solitary ,

what shall I do?

Either put off the fires of heart

or blow in the air..

One who feels its worth ,

your loyalty you offer..

What hides in your heart ,

you just make me aware

that now on my own the journey seems never ending...

What shall I do??

Was it you?

Was it you or some ray of light,

was it you or had some flower- bud smiled?

was it you or a rain of dreams,

was it you or had the clouds of happiness covered me?

was it you or some flower had blossomed,

was it you or had I just found a new world?

was it you or was there fragrance in the winds?

was it you or were there colors in all directions?

was it you or was there light in the paths,

was it you or were there songs echoing all around?

was it you or had I found all my destinations?

was it you or was it a time full of magic?

Every second

Every second , close in my heart,

you remain

Every evening , upon my eyes,

your memories flutter..

Every breath I take , I receive your fragrance,

each and every redolence,

brings a message..

the beat of my heart too,

sings this song

the joys of burning,

only the moths understand

Similarly , you keep me burning,

by continully entering my dreams...

I won't forget

I won't forget

I won't forget

These rituals , these promises, these relations

i won't forget

But come let's forget this world

and lose ourselves in our thoughts

Let's tune in to the nature and touch the sky

with the flow of time

this age will pass..

the moments we are going to live,

only they'll remain..

I'll become the last breath

and you become life

And i won't forget the relation

between life and breaths..

May there be rainfall

May there be fragranced courtyard

May the heart be a groom

May the heart be a bride

Lets's roam around like he wind

Come let's turn the paths

and not leave each other ever!

Desire

You have spread like the spring,

Let the air catch your fragrance,

Let my gaze go crazy,

Let this evening deepen a bit,

Let my heart be steady,

Let me live for a little while,

Let me take some sips of the intoxication,

Haven't said anything yet,

my heart isn't satiated yet!

Drop by drop

My eyes shed tears,

drop by drop,

in hopes of your return,

my beloved..

Thousabds of sorrows and this solitude

are all parts of love's disgrace

the star of my beauty spot

burns brightly like an ember

Even the henna on my hands is sullen

I am an incomplete story

I am an incomplete story

When you remember me,

come back to me..

the state that I am in without you,

come to me and see it for yourself..

My eyelashes are moist,

as my tears drip, sounding

like the jingle of an anklet

Lost and sullen..

Letters

The letters I wrote to you,

turned into beautiful slights in your memory..

Come morning, they turned into flowers,

Come night, they turned into stars..

A beautiful bud blossomed,

and I thought you were blusing.

A fragrance filled the air

and It seemed to me your near..

The sights are colorful

so as your charms

the way you gather yourself ,

the way you sigh,

the loneliness you feel ,

the way you leave me pinning!

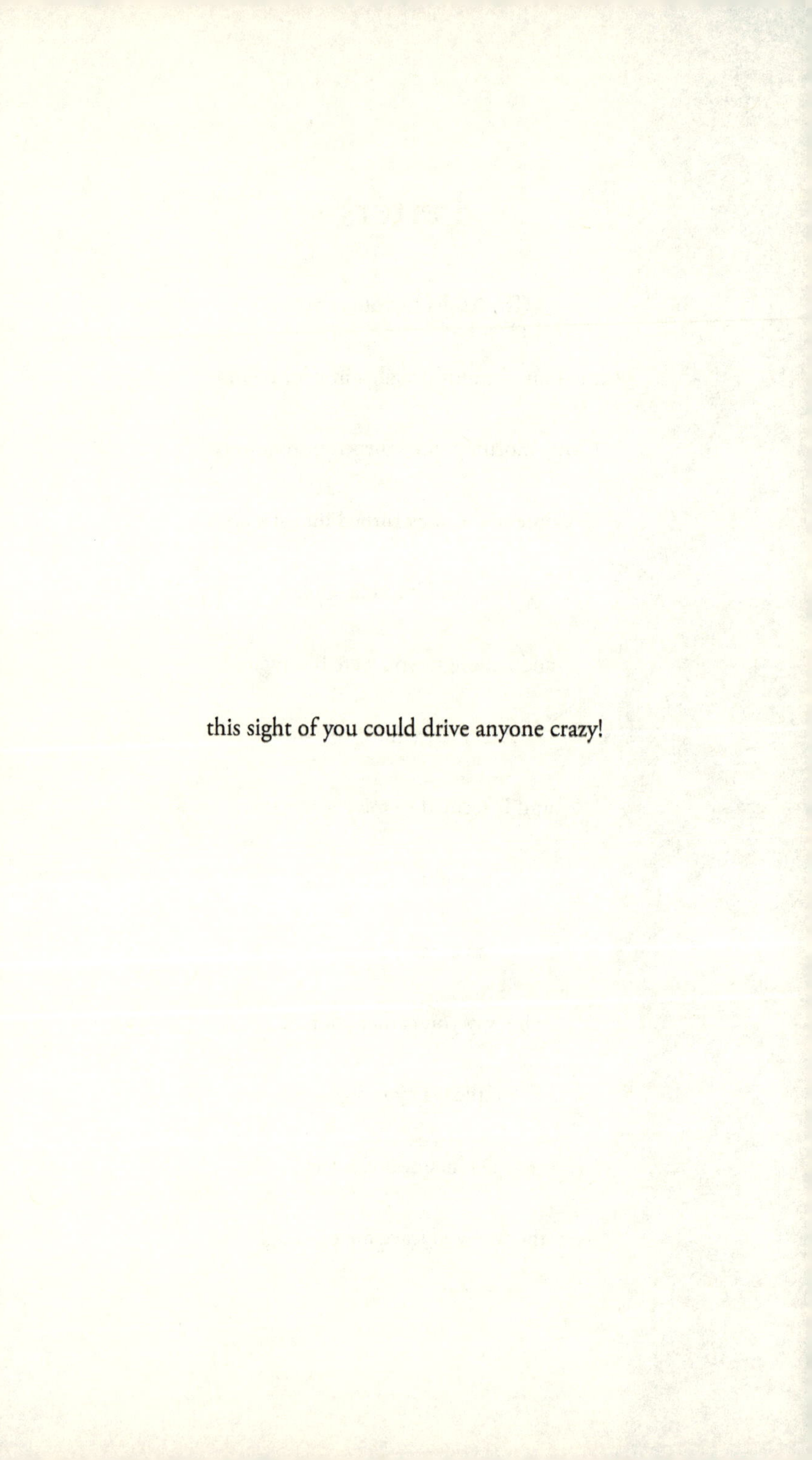

this sight of you could drive anyone crazy!

Paradise

Wherever you are, thats where

I want to be ,

you're the one heart beats for..

I am a traveller ,

you are my destination..

I am thirsty, you are the monsoon!

My world is held by the way

you look at me ,

My paradise lies in your embrace!

In your eyes

In your eyes,

there is a special kind of grace

What makes my heart

into a kite!

Your breath is that wind!

The day has come

a lucky one!

the one whom the whole world desires

is close to me

I have so much to say

but

still there are questions

in my heart

Everyday that I said in my dreams

Should I say that again or not!

Along with you

Along with you

some light has come..

Even the moon in front of your light

is nothing

but a light shadow

Condition

In the evening , I remember you,

it brings a storm,

and you are there in my memories..

every desire is kind of frank,

the heart is now lost in effrontery..

caravans of dreams

series of our talks ,

walk with me day and night ,

every moment the surrounding is lost in whisper..

Now don't ask me the condition of my heart!

Fragrance

Whether or not I am here,

this fragrance will remain..

As if a flower, as if a breeze

in our devoted garden..

I will fill our garden

gracefully with color

The color's of love..

and the sweet fragrance

will still fly from my hair,

whether autumn or spring

I will continue to blossom..

Gone

When I am gone,

when you pause

by my ashes as you walk

In a rainy moonlight

that is wet from my tears,

you will hear my call as you walk..

Faith is Love

Somewhere far away

when the day retires

The dusk sneaks up,

shyly like a bride

In the courtyard of my thoughts..

Someone lights up lamps of faith..

Sometimes when the breaths

become heavy meaninglessly

And the eyes moisten with tears

for no reason eminently

Just then someone overflowing

with love and feverishly

touches me lovingly

absolutely invisibly..

My heart knows all these deep secrets of mine..

How my dreams do actually take effect

Because these dreams of mine ,

they are only mine..

Even the shadows of my dreams never defect..

But the deep secrets of mine

are known to the one who lights up lamps of faith

in the courtyard of my thoughts!

Inside me

Still, somewhere inside me,

there is a little life remaining..

A new heartbeat came up,

I got to know that I am still alive..

A body that was scorching in the sun

has found a shade.

As if a miffed child

has got his smile back,

This is somewhat like my heart feels now..

Feels like my old wounds have healed..

My life was like a kite

cut from the strings,

Today is there, tomorrow maybe not,

was the story of everyday..

Some new bond is calling me from behind..

The worry about what is to come tomorrow

is not troubling me anymore..

Such a prickle is there in this moment..

Where had this moment been?

It's right in front of me now.

Let me feel it..

Do I embrace the happiness

or shed tears?

Structure

I saw my shadow on a wall

dancing like one in the rain!

The structure moved to let it stay,

the shadow gleamed fine all day!

They saw the shadow,
night and day;

called it a masterpiece,

with shades of grey!

The structure turned light ,

cold with continuous plight.

The shadow seemed a reality,

while the body searched for existence.

In the identity crisis,

truth got subdued and the lie pertained.

This seemed unfair,

but the world out there was fond of it.

To add to the confusion,

there was no truth.

There was just perception.

May we perceive beyond the truth!

Threads

Why does it feel like

someone is weaving dreams

with the threads of pashmina today..

How is that

when the valley echoes a new tune

of the rababb instrument...

How have the buds suddenly softened their attitudes..

How did the eyes that opened,

reveal new secrets and emotions!

How is it that someone's weaving their dreams

with pashmina threads today..

As a new young breeze is mixing some fresh sand,

a new young heart is choosing its new moments..

As new sunlight slips into new thresholds,

someone is saying silently..

Let me be your shadow,

Let me walk behind you,

Let me keep walking..

A couple of dewdrops

of went-a-wandering ,

they bloomed on the branches like pearls..

Without any worries

they mix around..

They meet in their thoughts ,

even when they seperate

And in the imagination,

they continued their meetings..

How is that when the valley echoes a new tune,

it stays afloat like a white cloud..

How is it that someone's weaving their dreams

with pashmina threads today!

Stairs Of Lifer

As far as the stairs of life go

I'll climb with you

Either it is the moment of happiness or sadness,

the sunlight or the shades,

I will always stand by your side..

I am not one of those who don't keep the promiises

and easily give up..

Neither I am one of those

who pretend to be truthful

but eventually tell lies..

Neither I am one those

who tell you that they

can bring you the stars from the skies..

I will only say

what i will be able to prove you.

I will live with you

and die alongside you..

Even there are moments

of happiness olr griefs,

the blazing suns or the dark shades,

I will always stand with you..

I don't promise you the forts..

It would be a small house instead..

I would not be able to earn millions

but we will manage with thousands instead..

I am not surely one of those

who will show you luxury dreams to have you..

I will only say that

I will be able to prove to you.

I will live with you

and die alongside you..

you will be a part of each success

that I shall achieve in this life

Being happy will become a habit for you,

and you will never shed a tear..

I am not one of them

who hold hands of their beloved first

and then step back at tough moments in life..

Neither I am one of such careless ones

who take away one sleep

but themselves sleep carefree..

Even there are moments of happiness or griefs,

the blazing sun or the dark shades,

I will stand wih you..

As far as the stairs of life go

I'll climb with you

I'll climb with you

If you truly

If you truly trust me,

give me all your sorrow..

Each tear that irks those eyes,

come, let me borrow.

If I make your troubles mine,

I'll be at ease..

If I hide your pain in my heart

I'll be at peace.

Every such thing that rakes you,

everything that makes you sad,

give it to me.

Let me know all that stakes you or breaks you..

Let me be the dawn that wakes you..

And let me be the eve

that makes you sleep in blissful reverie..

If I am a part of your life,

then why not a part of your strife?

Why don't you share your worries

And let me diminsh all miseries..

The angst that burns your heart,

of that let me be a part

Let there be no tears that rile...

These beautiful eyes for a while..

Keep the laughter alive in these eyes

and may these lips always smile...

But do give me all your sighs,

and give me all the pain that ails you..

For I'll never be the one who fails you.

If you truly trust me,

give me all your sorrow..

Each tear that irks those eyes,

come, let me borrow..

I told the stars about you

I told the stars about you..

The words I carefully hide,

underneath a peaceful sky,

finally of their weight tired,

I let them tonight fly.

Words of this astonish world,

that I long for you to hear,

at the stars I finally told,

How much i cherish you, dear.

I'll remember

I'll remember these moments for years..

If these seasons pass

then I'll request for them..

From the photos of these dreams

From the shackles of these memories

How will I free my heart from them?

Oh! i'll remember these moments for years.

Just for me

Sometimes , in my heart

a feeling emerges

that It's like you have been created

just for me..

Before, you dwelled among the stars somewhere..

And now , you have been called down to the earth

just for me..

Sometimes, in my heart a feeling emerges..

Hope

A heart as 'pure' as 'gold'..

A laughter sweet as a summer day..

A fire brighter than the sun..

But

I'm surrounded by walls I've made myself..

Every brick

An insecurity

No door

No escape

No hope

But when you look closer to see a crack

A small glimmer of hope

It's calling you

Will you step into the light?

Isolation

Living my peaceful life,

and watching as the chapters unfold..

I was never lonely

I prefer to be alone..

As the bright days, turn dark,

and the night gets more cold

I am not lonely

I am just alone..

As I read a book

while listening to the piano,

and burned all of the coal.

Maybe I am lonely

and left alone

As I feel life slipping away,

because I no longer wanted to hold.

i couldn't be lonely

and I am just alone..

Looking back , I realised that,

I wanted so much control..

I was the one who made myself lonely,

thats why, I was meant to be alone..

Once

Faded away

and burried thoughts

that are gray

and blurry.

Once light and hope

now darkness.

Once love and warmth

now malice.

Faded away,

forgotten,

once loved and kind

now... rotten

All I Own

Sleepless nights and tireless days

Still I write with things to say

To whom It may concern

I'll never know

By the time you read this

I'll be six feet below

But before I'm gone

I have to write

My last will and testament

It is my right

So I leave to you all I own

A pen

A paper

and this poem...

To the Unknown

To the unknown, I write this song

Speaking of me, but not so long

Don't know why, don't know who

But have faith in me

that it's for you..

I see the world and understand It's ways

I recommend to do whatever as you may

Neither gods nor devils,

name it who,

Let only soul of yous guide

to the real you,,

As you grow, you shall know,

world is full of people caring deep woe..

You are too, having struggle being part of it,

It is because you weren't supposed to fit..

To be the difference ,

follow the light

which shines within you

too bright!!

Notes

Life is a song

Pleasure is the hook

Pain is the chorus

The melody lives in every inch of time and space..

We all live in harmony with it

yet few can read it's notes..

Tomorrow won't come

Time stopped in a single moment

Once you gave you hand in my hand

Now I'll go wherever you'd go

I'll be on your right side,

you'd be on my left side..

I am the season you're the seasonal wind..

your face is accompanying me as a shadow

that's the situation nowadays

I am the morning and you're the sunlight

I am the mirror and you're the beauty

reflected on me..

Now..

Let's get lost somewhere

where the time would stop itself

Tomorrow won't come!

Slipping away

Between fingers are gaps of eternity;

The thumb moves to hold on..

to numbers

to time

to memories

Only that, it keeps slipping ,

like lost hankies , toothless childhood,

and lovers with rain drenched eyes..

Bloom

Everything will come back to life

and my heart will start to bloom again..

I am happier now,

each day that goes by

Still some memories are worthy to keep in heart

The last signs of season

will soon melt away..

yet some things will be remembered

everything will come back to life

and my heart will start to bloom once again!

That girl

She loved late nights,

when the owl hoots into the darkness,

when the moon shines like a diamond,

when the stars wink on the sky,

when the leaves rustle against the murmuring wind,

when the whole world sleeps,

and when no one hears her screaming

and crying into her pillow...

A Lady behind me

There is a lady behind me

Laughs with so many

But happy... I doubt with any

She smiles randomly

who knows

she screams so badly!

There is lady behind me

lives whole day and whole night

As nothing is wrong

says she don't care

The world says her rude

Who knows!

she is dead inside ....dude

Stuck

The mind gets tired

when looking for peace

when the pitcher of pain overflows..

The tears are lost and sit in silence

The wall of the mind

becomes a stone,

bringing a tide of laughter

Weave

When the body perishes

all perishes

But the threads of memory

are woven of enduring atoms

I will pick these particles

weave the threads ..

and I will meet you yet again!

Heaven

I am looking for that reality

which shines even in the extreme dark conditions..

I am looking for that love

which I left at your doorstep..

People of the world , try to understand the prayer

when one bows down ..

I am looking for that heaven

which you attain after death..

Questions

Your memories have kept me alive..

or else

the questions would have

killed me long time back..

Says

Sometimes a person without saying anything,

says everything..

You aren't an imagination

You are the living feeling

that runs in my heart as breath..

you are a promise

made to my soul

that rests on the foundation of faith..

you are my pride,

who introduced me

to the purity of love..